BOSTON MARATHON OR BUST:

a proven step-by-step program to help you achieve your *life*, *sports*, and *business* goals in record time

SCOTT SHARP ARMSTRONG

MORGAN JAMES PUBLISHING • NEW YORK

BOSTON MARATHON OR BUST:

ISBN: 978-1-60037-246-9 (Hardcover)
ISBN: 978-1-60037-245-2 (Paperback)

Published by:

MORGAN · JAMES
THE ENTREPRENEURIAL PUBLISHER™
www.morganjamespublishing.com

Morgan James Publishing, LLC
1225 Franklin Ave Ste 32
Garden City, NY 11530-1693
Toll Free 800-485-4943
www.MorganJamesPublishing.com

Cover/Interior Design by:
Rachel Campbell
rachel@r2cdesign.com

Habitat
for Humanity®
Peninsula
Building Partner

http://www.BoulderCoachingAcademy.com
Scott@BoulderCoachingAcademy.com

To all of you who have dreams.
Go for it!

ACKNOWLEDGEMENTS

THIS BOOK WOULD NOT HAVE BEEN POSSIBLE WITHOUT the dedication, support, and vision from those of you who shared in my dream and allowed me to create this very special contribution to the world.

First of all I would like to thank my wife Sarah for all her love and support and hanging in there with me until the end. I love you!

Secondly I would like to thank my parents for their support and encouragement over the years and believing in me and my big dream.

In addition, a special thanks to my sister-in-law, Eileen Armstrong, for your insight and creative ideas during our brain storming sessions. And most assuredly, I want to acknowledge and thank the best editor in the world, Dr. Patricia Ross. You are amazing.

Finally, a heartfelt appreciation is made to the following individuals who without their inspiration, friendship and help this book would not have been possible: Glenn Dietzel, Karen Merriam, Dr. Paul Gluch, Paul Jackson, Matt Moyer, and Linda McGrory.

TESTIMONIALS

"IN THAT GAP BETWEEN INSPIRATION AND ACTION, read *Boston Marathon or Bust* and set yourself up for the realization of your wildest dreams. If you're not inspired read it anyway and you will be!"

LORRAINE MOLLER
4 time Olympian and Bronze Medalist
Boston Marathon Winner

"I have attended over 500 motivational seminars around the United States. In one session with Scott Armstrong, I learned more than all the other 500 seminars combined! Nobody can connect and deliver like Scott. He is simply the best there is."

ORRIN HUDSON
Author and Achievement Strategy Expert

"I have read Scott's book and as a coach, entrepreneur and business owner I have found it to be very inspirational. From goal setting strategies to having faith and belief, his book is a step by step blue print how to make dreams a reality. It is a must read for anybody that desires their Gold-Medal in life. In fact, I was so impressed by the book that I gave it to my daughter to read."

Mark Plaatjes
Gold Medal Winner
Marathon World Championships

"As a performance psychology specialist, I've found Scott Armstrong's e-book *Boston Marathon or Bust* a must read for anyone who wants to live the life they've always dreamed about. Scott has taken the wisdom of the world's best success coaches and tells you how to apply it. His step-by-step approach provides the essential ingredients to succeed in any endeavor."

Dr. Paul Gluch
Stress Management Consultant
Costa Mesa, California

"Packed with concrete strategies for success and motivating principles which will get the reader to take action, Scott Armstrong has crafted a gem which will surely impact the lives of those who read it. The bonus is that Scott's own life and success are evidence of how powerfully his approach works!"

CAROLE WAGONHURST
Coach & Author
North Garden, Virginia

I highly recommend this book. Here's why:

As a coach, I've always had a hard time answering clients who asked how to go about "pulling down a dream, dusting it off, making a goal of it – and succeeding." I'd reply that to make a dream happen, you have to really want it, be convinced you deserve it, and then go for it! While all of this is correct, it failed to address the all-important question of "How?" In trying to evolve a better answer to that "how," I've read a lot about setting and achieving goals. Some authors used metaphors, some were theoretical, others a bit simplistic. None felt like they exactly fit my needs.

With *Boston Marathon or Bust*, Scott Armstrong tackles the "how" question in a way that is clear and totally repeatable. Scott uses his experiences in training for the Boston Marathon to take the reader step-by-step through the action plan he used to make his marathon dream come true. In the process, he shows how anyone can manifest any dream, by following the same plan.

As Scott makes abundantly clear: "there is no magic about achieving dreams." But instead of theory, Scott provides his readers with a workable action plan, one he's evolved through experience. And he shows how he's used his plan again and again to achieve success in his personal and professional life.

So for all the coaching clients who've moaned, "But Anne, do you REALLY think I have what it takes to do this?" I will now emphatically say, "Yes. Especially if you follow the plan outlined in *Boston Marathon or Bust.*"

ANNE HOLMES
President
Anne Holmes Associates
Galena, Illinois

"Scott is not only an exceptional coach, he's an exceptional human being. Being coached by Scott has been a life-changing experience of the highest order."

KAREN KNOWLER
The Raw Food Coach, U.K.

"Scott Armstrong has taught me more in four lessons than I have been able to come across in my entire life. Between the new daily habits, increased awareness, focus, and consistency of action, I know I am on a direct course to obtain all my goals and dreams. There will be no stopping me now that I have been shown the path to greatness."

PAUL BURGESS

Florida Real Estate Investor

"Scott Armstrong's coaching has lifted my life to a higher level in no time. Before I knew him I was frustrated, unfocused and underachieving. His expertise and enthusiasm have led me to achieve things I would never have imagined possible – he is absolutely top-notch!"

DR. ELIZABETH DRAYSON

Professor

University of Cambridge

"Scott Armstrong has been my coach, mentor and friend for the last two years. In that time I can truly say that his methods and ideas have changed my life for the better! He has had faith in me and my ideas even when I didn't. Scott is simply the best! Thank you, Scott!"

DAN SMITH

Owner

The PhotoSmith LLC

Lexington, Kentucky

"My name is Linda McGrory, and I started working with Scott about one year ago. Before that time, I was completely lacking in confidence, stuck in my comfort zone and incapable of moving forward to achieve my dreams. With Scott's patience, understanding and constant support, I have been able to realize that I do have something worthwhile to contribute and that I can be a success, but most importantly, Scott has helped me to take action. Thank you Scott, you have changed my life."

LINDA McGRORY

Author, Coach, Entrepreneur

Cornwall, U.K.

"All the great ones throughout time have had coaches. Do the research and you'll see the truth in that. If you are in the business of success, and the last time I checked who isn't, then Scott

Armstrong better be your coach. Scott will have you motivated and accomplishing things you thought were once impossible. Scott Armstrong, hands down, is one of the best mentors/coaches that I've ever worked with!"

STEVE GRZYMKOWSKI
Pipersville,PA

"Scott is truly amazing. So much enthusiasm, so dynamic, he walks his talk! Learn from him. Listen to him. Use him!! Scott will add so much to your life!" Go Scott go!!!"

JOSEPH COSTELLO
Dublin, Ireland

"Scott has served as my personal coach for over a year. The results have been astounding. When I began with Scott, I had just started a new consulting and coaching business. Even though I had over 28 years in management experience and my coaching certificate was in my hand, I felt uncertain and feared that I would not be successful. Scott focused on what was possible, and the change in me has been dramatic. Every day is now an exciting new opportunity for me and my business. Most important, my commitment to be focused, confident and effective in serving others as they seek to fulfill their dreams and performance goals is being realized beyond my expectations."

January H. Scott
President/CEO
JHS Solutions, LLC
Topeka, Kansas

"Scott Armstrong's strategies should be required for everyone who wants more freedom, greater achievement, and increased fulfillment in their life! Scott teaches you how to become clear on what you want and then conquer every obstacle to accomplish your goal. His methods are top-notch!"

Nick Wendowski
The HERO Maker™

Philadelphia, Pennsylvania

"Scott, I do not have the words to tell you how much your coaching has meant to me. Before I met you, I was self-employed, giving lectures and workshops on stress, but the business was not going very well. I had the choice between going back to a

9-5 job (I hated the thought) or getting some help. Luckily I found you. You helped me to succeed. The turning point came shortly after we started. My business got better and better. Now I am one of the leading stress experts in Denmark and soon going international. I have a flourishing business and can live my dreams! Thank you!"

BJAREN TOFTEGÅRD

Copenhagen, Denmark

"I began reading *Boston Marathon or Bust* with a little bit of skepticism. I know the importance of dreaming big dreams, and I'm also pretty adept at making those dreams happen. Because of that, I don't usually read self help books, but I was given Scott's book to read by my mother-in-law. I was amazed and very pleased to find that half way through the chapter on Goal Setting, I was hooked! I started using the plan that Scott laid out, and the results were spectacular! My business *immediately* started to boom. I was so impressed that I hired Scott as my coach. His insight, experience, and his great enthusiasm to help have truly helped me take my game to a new high level. Thanks Scott Sharp Armstrong for giving us a straight forward plan that not only motivates but is easy to follow too! You help make lives better and happier, and for that I applaud you!!!"

Patricia Springsteel
President/Executive Director
Learning Basics Training and Tutoring Company
Denver, Colorado

"Scott has been phenomenal in assisting me to find clarity in what I want to achieve in my life; he gave me a foundation to build on and then gave me the tools to show me how to focus and take action in order to move toward my goals and ultimately achieve them.

Scott delivers, and he is extremely generous in sharing his wealth of experience, knowledge and resources. What I like best about Scott is he genuinely cares about my success. I love his confidence in me. With Scott as my coach and mentor, I am UNSTOPPABLE!"

Julie Henderson
Canada

"I've known Scott Armstrong quite some time now, and I am impressed with the quality of his work. I had set some goals for myself, but for some reason they "just didn't happen". When I engaged Scott's services, I suddenly started to make major progress.

Scott has a way of getting you to move forward, without you feeling pressed. His coaching style is very "organic".

Although I live in Australia, I felt like I had face-to-face sessions with Scott; the distance was never an issue. His step-by-step approach and his gentle way of holding you accountable make Scott a great coach!

His latest book breathes the same approach. It's a must-read for anyone serious about making changes in their lives! I recognized a lot of what Scott and I discussed in our sessions. Good on ya, mate!"

MARC DE BRUIN
Master NLP Practitioner and Coach
Australia

TABLE OF CONTENTS

INTRODUCTION

"**Boston Marathon or Bust**" **is my attempt to put** into words an experience of a lifetime – qualifying for and running in the Boston Marathon. Like many of you I had a dream, but unlike most people, I lived mine. It wasn't easy, but the achievement of dreams isn't meant to be easy.

This book is a plan of action for anyone with a dream who is serious about making it come true. There is no magic about achieving dreams. It takes a plan and personal commitment to follow that plan. The basic plan is provided by me. The details of your plan are yours to fill in.

Most of all, the plan centers around what you do, not what you would like to do or say you are going to do. Also, it's attitude—attitude carries the day. Your attitude has to be a positive one. You must believe in yourself.

All of the basic steps in the plan are important. They include: The Power of Beliefs; Goal Setting; Visualization; Affirmations;

Persistence; Find a Mentor or Coach. The one step that seems to separate those individuals who actually succeed from those who just come close is having the guidance of a Mentor/Coach.

Coaches or Mentors provide that little "extra" needed to truly succeed. Whether it's a personal or professional goal you wish to reach, a coach provides you with many things: a mirror for you as you take the journey to your dream; a person to whom you are accountable; the experience of having been there and the wisdom born of that experience; the glue that melds your past experiences, present knowledge, and future plans; a sounding board; advice from an expert. Most important, a Mentor or a Coach is someone with whom to celebrate when your goal is reached!

There is no doubt that following this plan will lead you along the path to success just like it has done for me over and over again both in my personal and in my professional life.

A PERSONAL NOTE

I walk my talk. In fact, I was walking my talk even before I realized that I had a plan. Let me explain where I am coming from. At nine years of age my parents gave me a gum-ball machine. I found the local gum-ball machine distributor and bought three additional machines. The word got out and the neighbourhood kids came streaming through the kitchen on a daily basis. I made hundreds of dollars with my very first business. The entrepreneurial spirit was born!

The plan I present to you here evolved through experience along with one other ingredient. Paul Jackson, a friend of mine, talks about wisdom using the following formula:

KNOWLEDGE + EXPERIENCE + REFLECTION = WISDOM

I agree with him, and I found that reflection is by far the most important part of the equation. Without reflection, experience is not cumulative. It is reflection that allows me to understand myself and motivates me to help you.

My drive for achievement wasn't restricted to my professional life. Athletics and personal fitness have always been a very large part of my life. While I enjoy many sports, I have always been most enthusiastic about long-distance running. I've completed over a dozen marathons, and I consider qualifying for and finishing the Boston Marathon one of my greatest personal success stories.

My personal and professional development included mentors and coaches like Brian Tracy, Jim Rohn, Tom Hopkins, Zig Ziglar, Wayne Dyer, Mike Litman, Tony Robbins and Toastmasters. They all helped to shape who I am today, and for that I'm most grateful.

I did not do it alone. And you won't either. Allow me to be on your list of Mentors/Coaches that propel you to personal and professional success in whatever you choose to do.

Read on!

Enjoy!

Act!

SINCERELY,

Scott Armstrong

"If you believe you can, you probably can. If you believe you won't, you most assuredly won't. Belief is the ignition switch that gets you off the launching pad."

— DENIS WAITLEY

CHAPTER ONE

The Power of Beliefs

Without belief, I would never have achieved my dreams. It is what has kept me pursuing my dreams when things have not necessarily been going well. I have always believed in myself and my talents and that I could accomplish my dreams.

WHAT IS A BELIEF?

> *"One person with a belief is equal to a force of ninety nine who only have an interest."*
>
> **– JOHN STUART MILL**

A belief is any guiding principle, dictum, faith or passion that can provide direction and meaning in life. When we trust something is true, that belief delivers a strong command to the brain to visualize what we are convinced will occur while simultaneously changing our subconscious thought patterns.

Having a strong belief can be your most powerful tool in bringing great things into your life. A series of strong beliefs can empower you so you can achieve almost any goal that you set for yourself. Once you set your goal and you truly believe you can accomplish it, your nervous system and brain come into play and make it work. Throughout history, people who have had strong beliefs have accomplished things many people thought were previously impossible.

To change your behaviors, it is important to examine your current belief system and be open to changing what doesn't work. The first step in changing your belief system is to find people who have done what you want to accomplish. Study their belief systems and incorporate them into your own belief structure. As these wise folks know, success leaves clues.

> *"Whether you believe you can do a thing or not,*
> *you are correct."*
>
> – HENRY FORD

THE FIRE WALK

It is important in your life to do things that will challenge your established belief patterns and get you out of your comfort zone.

The event in my life that took my belief system to an entirely new level was the fire walk experience with Tony Robbins. As you may already know, Tony Robbins is a well known motivational speaker and the father of the Life Coaching movement. On the first day of his seminar, participants walk across a bed of hot coals. I will never forget signing the waiver form right before the event which stated that Robbins Research International was not responsible for any bodily harm — noting that the coals can reach temperatures up to 1,200 degrees! Trying to stay positive, I thought to myself at the time, "If I don't get through the fire walk successfully, I could always become a professional stump dancer!"

In the end I made it through unharmed, and that successful walk across a twenty foot bed of hot coals took my belief system as well as my mental game to an entirely new level. The fire walk also demonstrated to me that I can trust myself and have the ability to use *my* mind over physical obstacles. It removed any doubt about my ability to do anything I thought was difficult or impossible. That is why I now believe that if I could get myself to walk over red hot coals, the world is open and waiting for me to achieve things I previously thought I could not.

There is a story about Thomas Edison that talks about his beliefs and his ability to deal with failure after failure. Most people fail a couple of times and give up. Edison, who took more than ten years and twenty thousand experiments to invent a light, durable, efficient battery, tells of someone questioning his route: "Mr. Edison, you have failed twenty thousand times, what makes you think you will get results?" To which Edison replied "Results? Why, I've got a lot of results. I know twenty thousand things that don't work."

"Believe Big. The size of your success is determined by the size of your belief. Think little goals and expect little achievements. Think big goals and win big success. Remember this, too! Big ideas and big plans are often easier — certainly no more difficult — than small ideas and small plans."

– David J. Schwartz

Where do beliefs come from?

Beliefs come from different events in your life. We all have experiences that we won't forget. We each have events in our own lives that create or alter the perceptions we have of our own world. A good way to reconstruct or bolster a belief structure is through seeking additional knowledge. By reading books on how others have achieved incredible accomplishments, you will help shift your belief system relating to what is possible. This will eventually help you succeed. Also, talking to anyone you can find who has accomplished what you wish to accomplish adds to your knowledge base. Learn as much as you can from others' experiences. Most people enjoy talking about their successes and sharing the knowledge they have gained.

USE PAST RESULTS

Your past results are another way to redefine and strengthen your belief system. There is a wise saying: "Success breeds success." When I first started running, I never ran more than five miles. Then one day, one of my friends said, "You need to go for a gutsy run!" I gave it a try and pushed my comfort zone. I went on a ten mile "gutsy" run and I was hooked on long-distance running. This shifted my belief system that related to how far I could push my body and what I was capable of accomplishing. With that run under my belt, I continued to push myself and eventually accomplished getting that medal around my neck at the end of the Boston Marathon.

STICK WITH THE POSITIVE

If you want to succeed, it is important to choose what beliefs you wish to change first, and to seek out those who can help you with your undertaking. As you establish your revised belief system, it is critical that you surround yourself with as many positive and motivational people as possible. Then, you need to continually work toward being involved in events that will bolster your new way of perceiving the world. This will help filter out all the negatives that might come your way. You see, your belief system doesn't differentiate or judge; it simply accepts as truth what you feed it. The power of belief works just as efficiently on your thoughts of self-doubt and limitations as it does on success and achievement.

The question is: how do you change your belief system of negative thoughts? One technique that is helpful when you come across negative thoughts is to say, "Cancel." As Earl Nightingale said: "you become what you think about." This is why it is so important to guard the thoughts of your mind. Remember that our belief system is brought on by repetition of thoughts and by past experiences.

"If you believe you can, you probably can. If you believe you won't, you most assuredly won't. Belief is the ignition switch that gets you off the launching pad."

— Denis Waitley

Count your Successes, Past and Future

"If you develop the absolute sense of certainty that powerful beliefs provide, then you can get yourself to

*accomplish virtually anything, including those things
that other people are certain are impossible."*

— TONY ROBBINS

Our beliefs come from our successes, small or large. One powerful way to change your belief system is to make a list of all your successes, small or large. List out the characteristics that made those successes possible. Then use visualization techniques to visualize yourself having those characteristics you desire. Imagine your new belief system is established and act upon it!

Belief has played a big part in top performances in sports. Billy Jean King said more matches are won internally then externally. I can relate to her. In my experience, the last seven or eight miles of a marathon is all mental. The marathon is won in your mind and with your beliefs, and those last miles are the true test of the race. I went into my races with this mind-set, and it was extremely helpful. I stuck with my mental game plan and believed I could accomplish my goal.

*"Gold medals are not just won on superior talent
alone. It is the ability to keep a strong mind and truly
believe in yourself and your ability regardless of the
conditions and the opposition."*

— IWAN THOMAS

"...Sting like a bee..."

There is a classic story about when boxing heavy weight champion Mohammed Ali fought George Foreman in a boxing match that was called the "Rumble in the Jungle." Ali had been beaten twice and many people believed that at age thirty-two he was past his prime. The boxing world thought he would be brutally beaten by this much younger, stronger, and seemingly more dangerous man. Even Ali's training camp had serious doubts. However, Ali had a different idea; he told the world he was going to win and said in an interview: "I am thirty-two; the stage is set, my legs haven't gone. I am still strong. I am the fastest, the prettiest, the most scientific, the classiest boxer. I am the greatest fighter of all time!" He won the fight in forceful style, shocking and pleasing millions of people! Ali had an established belief system that allowed him to tune out the negative and focus on the positive. That belief system came from past experiences of success and from surrounding himself with people who offered useful advice as well as shared their enthusiasm for his goals.

What next?

Once you have taken an inventory of your past successes and have made a list of the beliefs you want to change, you will need to create and follow a program that includes Goal Setting, Visualization,

Affirmation and establishing a relationship with a Mentor or Coach. I have briefly touched upon a few of these essentials here and will go into greater depths in the following chapters.

"Believe deep down in your heart that you're destined to do great things."

— JOE PATERNO

"All who have accomplished great things have had a great aim, have fixed their gaze on a goal which was high, one which sometimes seemed impossible."

— **ORISON SWETT MARDEN**

CHAPTER TWO

Goal Setting

"The reason most people never reach their goals is that they don't define them, learn about them or even seriously consider them as believable or achievable. Winners can tell you where they are going, what they plan to do along the way, and who will be sharing the adventure with them."

— **DENIS WAITLEY**

M arathon runners—except Olympians—soon learn that a marathon is not about who wins the race. It is about each person achieving their own personal victories.

The cornerstone of achieving your dreams is learning how to set goals. Setting goals in all areas of your life is important on your road to success. The goal you tackle first is to clearly identify your purpose, meaning your cornerstone goal, which comes to light when you ask yourself the question "Which goal, if accomplished, would do the most to help me achieve all of my other goals?" When you formulate a clear and focused purpose, many forces in the mental universe begin to work for you. You begin to move very quickly towards your goal and knock down any walls in your way.

"When you are inspired by some great purpose, some extraordinary project, all your thoughts break their bonds; your mind transcends limitation, your consciousness expands in every direction, and you find yourself in a new, great wonderful world. Dormant forces, faculties and talents become alive, and you discover yourself to be a greater person by far than you ever dreamed yourself to be."

— PATANJALI

The process for selecting your purpose begins by asking yourself some elementary questions:

✳ *Attitude:* Is there any part of my mind-set that is holding me back?

✳ *Career:* What levels do I want to reach in my career?

✳ *Education:* Do I want to further my education?

✳ *Family:* How do I want to be viewed by my partner or family?

✳ *Financial:* How much do I want to be earning? How much do I want to have in the bank? What is the amount of money I need to be financially free?

✳ *Physical:* Are there any athletic goals I want to accomplish? Do I want to start to eat better and take care of my body? What is my ideal weight?

✳ *Spiritual Goals:* Do I want to improve the relationship with my creator? What kind of person do I want to become?

✳ *Community Goals:* Do I want to spend more time giving back to the community?

✳ *Material Goals:* What do I want to have?

✳ *Travel Goals:* What places do I want to travel to?

One of the most important skills that I learned while achieving my dream was goal-setting. Goal-setting has been called the master skill of success. This one skill, if you master it, can make incredible changes in your life. Take for example Yale University's renowned goal-setting study initiated in 1953. Researchers surveyed the graduating class and discovered that only three percent had written goals. Twenty years later, Yale surveyed this same class and learned that the three percent with clearly written goals was worth more in financial terms than the ninety seven percent combined. This study shows how powerful goal setting can be. Intense goal orientation is an essential characteristic of all high achieving men and women.

Most people training for their first marathon set their goal toward finishing. If they succeed at this most basic of marathoning goals, they may use the confidence they have acquired and decide to set their sights on breaking through a specific time limit, such as four hours for the 26.2 mile race. Having accomplished this goal, and gaining additional self-belief, they could become more aggressive in their goal setting and attempt to qualify for the Boston Marathon. As I have said, one of the biggest goals I have ever set was to qualify for and run in the Boston Marathon. To qualify, I needed to run less than a 3:10, thereby becoming part of an elite class of runners who are considered the very top percent of marathoners in the world. I had the added incentive that if I qualified my Dad said he would fly me to Boston from Boulder! Even better!

Once I had set my goal to qualify, it became complicated by the fact that the race I would run in was the hundredth running of the Boston Marathon! Virtually every serious marathoner was trying to qualify for this one-time event. This often happens with goals. Obstacles will arise that may force you to make an even greater effort, but you have to stick to your goal and overcome these complications. In this case, I needed to get more serious about the goal setting process. I wanted to be part of this once-in-a-lifetime event, and I decided after twelve years of marathoning this was "make it or break it" time. Boston or Bust!

THE GOAL PROCESS

"Remember, what you get by reaching your destination isn't nearly as important as what you become by reaching your goals—what you will become is the winner you were born to be!"

– ZIG ZIGLAR

My first goal was to hire a marathon coach. I wanted to find one of the best marathon coaches available so that person could help me achieve my goal. After a great deal of research and networking, I found a coach who was a former United States Olympic marathoner.

My next goal was to find a fast, flat qualifying course. I spoke to a lot of marathoners and everyone agreed my best chance was to run the Chicago Marathon. Many of the previous marathons I had run were hilly which makes it more difficult to run your fastest time.

"It sometimes seems that an intense desire creates not only its own opportunities, but its own talents."

– ERIC HOFFER

Get Strategic

Let me take a moment here to share with you the goal-setting strategies I used to help achieve my big dream.

Write it down.   When I am working toward a goal, I put it down on paper. Studies have shown that, when you write a goal down, the chance of you achieving it are one thousand times greater than if you didn't write it down at all. I don't know about you, but I really like those odds! When you write your goals down, it opens up the neural pathways to your brain conditioning your mind to receive these positive messages.

Detail it.   Writing your goals out in detail is very important as well. By doing this you are giving your subconscious mind a detailed set of instructions to work on. The more information you give your subconscious, the clearer the final outcome becomes. The more precise the outcome, the more efficient the subconscious mind can become.

Everyday.   The next key step is to write your goals down every day. This habit of writing your goals every day will help strengthen your neural pathways and help you establish clear/focused thinking. The more focused and clear you are about a goal, the greater chance you have to achieve them. Another wise saying goes: "repetition is the mother of skill."

MAKE IT POSITIVE. Goals should be stated in the positive and not in the negative. The more positive instruction you give your subconscious mind, the more positive results you will get. It is important to stay away from negative thoughts and negative people.

QUANTIFY IT. When you are setting your goals you need to be precise. Set a precise goal by putting in dates, times and comments so you can measure your achievement. If you do this, you will know exactly when you achieved your goal and take complete satisfaction from achieving it. To bolster your self-confidence, you may apply this to shorter term goals that lead to your long-term goal. For example, my 1st goal, as I stated earlier, was a sub 3:10 finishing time in Chicago. This goal was precise and clear. In addition, when you write down your goals, it crystallizes them and gives them force! Every day when I wrote my goals, I would write, "I ran a sub 3:10 in Chicago. I qualified for Boston." Other examples would be "I weigh x amount;" "I drive a new Silver 320 Class Mercedes Benz," etc. This is using your end desires to create your written goal. You may also use interim goals in this way as well. For example, if you want to run a marathon, you write goals for all the steps involved: the longer runs, the timed workouts, the speed workouts.

"Crystallize your goals. Make a plan for achieving them and set yourself a deadline. Then, with supreme

confidence, determination and disregard for obstacles
and other people's criticisms carry out your plan. "

— PAUL MEYER

Belief is essential when it comes to goal setting. Chapter One helps you create a successful belief system. Here, you add to that skill because, in order to activate your subconscious mind, you must believe it is possible for you to achieve your goal. You must have faith that you deserve your goal and that it will come to you. There is an amazing testimonial to the power of belief that I can relate to because it has to do with running. Roger Bannister had a belief that he could run a sub four-minute mile even though no-one at the time thought it was possible. Through him, the first sub four mile became a reality. Then, unbelievable as it may seem, Bannister's record only stood for 46 days before someone broke it! Once he proved that it could be done, many others were able to do it. Within two years more than 50 people ran a sub four-mile mark. Since then, thousands have run a sub four mile including many high school students. It is amazing what the human belief system can accomplish!

"All who have accomplished great things have had a
great aim, have fixed their gaze on a goal which was
high, one which sometimes seemed impossible. "

— ORISON SWETT MARDEN

It's like with Potato Chips: "You can't have just one…"

Continuous goal setting is important to your success and happiness. It is critical to build on your success and to get in the habit of continually setting goals. Make it a positive addiction. When you work toward achieving a goal, it brings excitement in your life and gets the endorphins going. This type of exhilarating experience will leave you with the desire for more. It is important to use that excitement and focus it on other goals. Once I achieved my goal of qualifying for and then running in Boston, I was very excited to set other challenging goals. You need to keep the momentum going and develop these good habits. Remember: people form habits and habits form futures!

Developing desire is another important trait to have on your goal-setting journey. What desire will do is knock down those walls that are called fear. Some say that fear stands for "false evidence appearing real," or "forget everything and run." Developing an intense burning desire will help you conquer fear and help you achieve your goals and dreams. I had an extremely intense, burning desire to qualify for the Boston Marathon. I had a "fire in the belly" that would not go away. It took me many years to achieve this goal, but the main reason I was able to accomplish it was I never lost that burning desire. If you can establish that burning desire, you can accomplish just about any goal that you set.

*"Desire is the starting point of all achievement,
not hope, not a wish, but a keen pulsating desire
which transcends everything."*

— Napoleon Hill

What's in it for me?

When setting your goals list all the ways you will benefit from accomplishing your goals. You have to ask yourself **why** you are doing this. I learned from Jim Rohn that you can achieve almost any goal if you have a big enough "why." When you list your "whys" it helps build that burning desire and move you forward rapidly toward your goals. The bigger the list of "whys," the more motivated you will be to accomplish you goals.

When you list your reasons, they must be inspiring. It is important to take the time and make the effort to develop a comprehensive list of reasons for accomplishing your goal. This fortifies your resolve and makes it next to impossible not to accomplish your goal. When the going gets tough and you reach those obstacles, the "why" has to be strong enough to move you forward. With a strong enough why, nothing will stop you. You will be able to break down any wall that you come up against.

"A man can bear any 'how'
if he has a big enough 'why.'"

— FRIEDRICH NIETSZCHE

To make sure your goals arc complete and are on track you should define them with the SMART formula. SMART stands for **S**pecific, **M**easurable, **A**ttainable, **R**ealistic, and **T**ime stamped.

BE SPECIFIC. Goals should be straight forward and emphasize what you want to happen. Specifics help us to be clear about what we are going to do. To set a specific goal you must answer the "W" questions.

❋ *Who?* Name those who are involved?

❋ *What?* List what you want to accomplish.

❋ *Where?* Identify a location.

❋ *When?* Establish a time frame.

❋ *Which?* Identify the requirements and constraints.

❋ *Why?* List specific reasons, purposes, or benefits for accomplishing the goal.

MAKE IT MEASURABLE. Identify criteria for measuring progress toward the attainment of each goal you set. When you measure your progress, it will help you stay on track and keep you focused.

HOW IS IT ATTAINABLE? When you identify goals that are important to you, you begin to figure out ways you can make them come true. You develop the attitudes, abilities, skills and financial capacity to reach them. You begin seeing previously overlooked opportunities to bring yourself closer to the achievement of your goals. A goal needs to stretch you slightly. You must feel that you can do it and that it will require a real commitment from you.

THE R STANDS FOR REALISTIC. Your goals must be realistic. Reach for the stars, but those stars must align with your resources, knowledge and time. Keep all your goals within the realm of the "possible." It would not be a realistic goal for me to be a Noble prize winning chemist, for example, because I am not interested nor am I good at chemistry. I aimed very high when I made the goal of qualifying for the Boston Marathon, but it was also realistic for me to do that because I have the talent for and the capability of being a long distance runner.

THE T STANDS FOR TIME STAMPED. It is very important to put some sort of deadline on your goals. Write them down on paper. Put them on your calendar and remind yourself daily of your commitment, your goals, and your actions.

If you follow the **SMART** formula for your goals, there will be no boundaries on what you can accomplish. This SMART method has worked for many people, and I am sure it will work for you!

"Goals give you more than a reason to get up in the morning; they are an incentive to keep you going all day. Goals tend to tap the deeper resources and draw the best out of life."

– HARVEY MACKAY

*"Formulate and stamp indelibly on your mind
a mental picture of yourself as succeeding. Hold
this picture tenaciously. Never permit it to fade.
Your mind will seek to develop the picture."*

– NORMAN VINCENT PEALE

CHAPTER THREE

Visualization

Visualization is one the most important things you can do to reach your goals and dreams. Performing my daily visualization exercises has allowed me to achieve several life goals. Visualization was a key component in helping me to qualify for and run in Boston.

Visualization is a powerful tool for building self confidence. With visualization, you see in your mind's eye the accomplishment or goal that you want to achieve. By visualizing each step in vivid detail, you change your perception of your capabilities by positively reinforcing the brain's pathways. The brain then delivers messages to the rest of your body that enable you to mentally and physically tackle the task at hand. In my case, I visualized twice a day my 26.2 mile race from a calm, calculated start to a triumphant finish. This technique may be used for both physically and mentally challenging goals.

"Ordinary people believe only in the possible.
Extraordinary people visualize not what is possible or
probable, but rather what is impossible.
And by visualizing the impossible, they begin to
see it as possible."

— CHERIE CARTER-SCOTT

Visualization has been used by athletes for many years and has been responsible for many world-record performances. One study I came across regarding visualization was by Charles Garfield, an expert on peak performance, who has done extensive research on this topic. His research has shown that all peak performers have one thing in common. They all use visualization techniques to help improve their performance. When these top performers use visualization to accomplish a goal they:

❋ SEE IT

❋ FEEL IT

❋ LIVE THE EXPERIENCE MENTALLY

❋ ACHIEVE IT

By visualizing your goals, you will change the hardwiring in your brain and you will enhance your self confidence. By living and reliving your dreams in your thoughts every day, you change your brain's patterns and eliminate the "I'm not sure I can do...."

thought patterns, and replace them with "I will do...." You will feel your self-confidence growing — visualization by visualization, day by day, goal by goal.

BOSTON OR BUST

I have been offering my experience of qualifying for and then running in the Boston Marathon as an example because both are difficult tasks. To some, even qualifying for the event seems unattainable because only a very small percentage of the marathoning community is capable of achieving the time necessary to qualify. When I was practicing my visualization techniques for my goal, it gave me added self-confidence. The more I visualized my desired outcome for the race, the more confident I felt I could accomplish my goal!

> *"See things as you would have them be
> instead of as they are."*
>
> **– ROBERT COLLIER**

Here are some of the visualization techniques that I used to help me achieve my dream:

* ❋ I started by visualizing, in detail, every aspect of the qualifying race in Chicago.

* I visualized running effortlessly, breathing smoothly, and feeling light weight.

* I could see each mile marker along the 26.2 mile course along with the exact times that I needed.

* At the finish line, I could see the finish clock with the time I needed to qualify.

* I could vividly see the spectators' faces, cheering me on to my big finish.

* I could see my wife's face with the most incredible look because she knew how badly I wanted to accomplish my dream.

* After finishing the race I could see myself giving high fives to the crowd and telling them I had just qualified for Boston!

Remember, the more rich and vivid the details that you can visualize, the better visualization will work for you.

> *"Formulate and stamp indelibly on your mind*
> *a mental picture of yourself as succeeding. Hold*
> *this picture tenaciously. Never permit it to fade.*
> *Your mind will seek to develop the picture."*

— NORMAN VINCENT PEALE

APPLY IT TO NON-ATHLETIC ENDEAVORS

Visualization can work for many different areas in your life. One of the areas of my life where it became very beneficial was as a member of Toastmasters International. Toastmasters International is an excellent program to help overcome the fear of speaking in public. Studies have shown that people's biggest fear in life is public speaking. The number two fear is death. Seinfeld, the comedian, put it best when he said that at a funeral most people would rather be in the casket than giving the eulogy.

During my three year membership, I learned many good visualization techniques that were helpful in improving my public speaking abilities. For any public speaking situation, I would visualize:

* *Standing* at the podium relaxed, poised, and breathing slowly.

* *Speaking* with confidence and having great eye contact.

* The audience *listening* attentively and looking captivated.

* *Receiving* a standing ovation with tremendous enthusiasm upon the completion of my speech.

Visualization is a very powerful technique. If you practice it, the results will amaze you. It is important that you do it twice a day to maximize your results.

Apply it to Sales

My sales career has benefited from visualization as well. To start my day, the first thing I do in the morning is visualize how I want my day to go. I visualize my sales calls going well. I see my daily, monthly and yearly sales goals very clearly. I see myself receiving the bonus for reaching my goals.

In your career, whatever it may be, see yourself getting that promotion or big raise you always wanted. See it clearly, vividly, relentlessly, over and over again.

My life goals are not limited to athletics or earning money. In my morning visualization ritual, I see how I want <u>all</u> aspects of my day to go. I see all the things I want to happen in <u>all areas</u> of my life: spiritually, emotionally, financially, as well as the material things I want in my life. I do this again right before I go to bed at night. I do this everyday because I believe in the saying that "people form habits and habits form futures."

*"Cherish your visions and your dreams, as they are
the children of your soul, the blueprints
of your ultimate achievements."*

— NAPOLEON HILL

HOW DO YOU PRACTICE?

When you practice your visualization exercises, there are certain steps and techniques you should follow to get the most out of it.

Start by totally relaxing your mind and body.

* ❋ *Breathe rhythmically* and deeply several times.

* ❋ *Take a minute* or two to relax your body starting with your toes and working your way to your head.

Next, start visualizing your goals as accomplished. Picture yourself already in possession of what you desire. As an example, if you want a new car, visualize this new car in detail. Use your imagination and involve the five senses of sight, smell, hearing, touch, taste. Put feeling and emotion into what you are doing. Smell the new leather. Feel the smooth paint job. Hear the brand new stereo. By doing this twice a day, you are sending positive energy into the universe. When you make this a habit, the law of attraction starts going into effect and more abundance will start appearing in your life. As Jim Rohn says, whatever you are moving towards is moving towards you.

What to do about the negative thoughts?

Negative thoughts may arise during the day. It is important to replace them as quickly as you can with a positive one. A good technique to use is the "Cancel technique." When a negative thought comes into your mind, immediately say:

"CANCEL"

and replace it with a positive thought.

Some inspiring examples

Visualization worked very well for two famous Olympians. Joan Benoit Samuelson employed such techniques in 1984 when she won the U.S. Olympic marathon, shortly after recovering from knee surgery. Grete Waitz of Norway, who had won all seven marathons she'd entered and had beaten Benoit in 10 of 11 races, was favored to win the gold medal in the first Olympic women's marathon in 1984. However, Benoit took the lead just 3 miles into the race and never gave it up. She recalled the finish: "When I came into the stadium and saw all the colors and everything, I told myself, 'Listen, just look straight ahead because if you don't you're probably going to faint.'" She kept her mind steady from start to finish. She saw it, felt it, experienced it mentally, and then did it.

When Bruce Jenner was training for the Olympics, he found visualization extended into his dream life. Several times, he saw himself crossing the finish in the 1,500 meters, the final event of the decathlon. Each time he was victorious. He said when the Olympics dream did come true, the moment felt oddly familiar. He saw it, felt it, experienced it mentally, and then did it with the feeling of familiarity. Bruce Jenner strengthened his neuro pathways and used that strength to coordinate his mind and body to achieve his dream. The more you do the exercises, the more visualization will help you in your particular activity.

"Obstacles are those frightful things you see when you take your eyes off your goal."

– HENRY FORD

"It's the repetition of affirmations that leads to belief.
And once that belief becomes a deep conviction,
things begin to happen."

– CLAUDE M. BRISTOL

CHAPTER FOUR

Affirmations (Self Talk)

*"We cannot always control our thoughts, but we
can control our words, and repetition impresses
the subconscious, and we are then master
of the situation."*

— FLORENCE SCOVEL SHINN

Affirmation, or self talk, is the next layer in the
process of accomplishing your life goals. Once you
have established your goals, have begun work on
reconstructing your belief system, and have mastered visualization,
the next piece is to practice affirmation.

FLICK THE LITTLE DOUBTER MAN OFF YOUR SHOULDER

Many of us have seen on TV or in movies the embodiment of a
character's self doubt as a little devil or doubting man perched on

that character's shoulder. The little man whispers negative thoughts to the character, attempting to get him or her to fail. We all have that little doubter man living on our shoulder, but what you need to do is flick him off, and you do it with affirmations.

An affirmation is similar to a chant. You use it to make a positive statement of fact or belief to yourself, that, when repeated enough, will keep you on track toward your goals. When you have doubts springing up, first say to yourself "Cancel," and then start repeating your affirmation to yourself.

Here are some tips on creating and using affirmations:

BEGIN WITH "I." The most important aspect of an affirmation is that you need to make it personal and it needs to start with "I."

PRESENT TENSE. Affirmations should be in the present tense. Keep the statement in the moment. By keeping it in the present tense, your subconscious can go to work on it immediately.

BE CONCISE. Affirmations should be in short powerful sentences. Your subconscious mind needs a clear message so stay away from long drawn-out sentences. Clarity is power.

REPEAT, REPEAT, REPEAT. You need to repeat your affirmations as often as possible. Ideally you want to do this twice a day, once when you get up in the morning, and then before you go to bed at night. When you do this before going to bed, you give your subconscious plenty of time to work on this key rewiring of your thought process. Take about forty-five to sixty seconds for each affirmation. Keep repeating them with feeling. The more feeling you put into your affirmations the sooner you're going to get results.

Some examples of affirmation might be:

❋ "I earn X amount of money."

❋ "I weigh 150 pounds."

❋ "I eat only healthy foods."

❋ "I am on the road to financial responsibility."

Studies by psychologists and neuroscientists have concluded that every person in the world has ongoing dialog or self-talk of between 150 and 300 words a minute. This works out to be between 45,000 and 51,000 thoughts day. It is vitally important to use all these thoughts in a positive way. Keep the positive thoughts in and the negative thoughts out of your mind.

"You become what you think about.."

— **Earl Nightingale**

When you allow a negative thought to enter into your mind, you reinforce a negative belief. If you want to change a negative belief you need to recondition your neural pathways. The key to blocking out negative thoughts and replacing them with positive thought patterns is by using affirmations. Use those several thousand thoughts per day to build yourself up, not tear yourself down.

"It's the repetition of affirmations that leads to belief.
And once that belief becomes a deep conviction,
things begin to happen."

– Claude M. Bristol

So, the basic plan up to this point is:

❋ Set your goals.

❋ Change your beliefs.

❋ Visualize.

❋ Affirm, Affirm, and Affirm again.

Flicking my own doubter man off at a critical time

Having used the affirmation technique along with the other techniques I have explained benefited me tremendously during my bid for a spot in the Boston Marathon. When I was training for the qualifying marathon, I used this affirmation technique. Doing affirmations on a daily basis was most helpful while trying to achieve my dream. My neural pathways had been reconstructed, and my self-confidence was high. But all that work was about to be put to the test....

For my qualifying race in Chicago, I was in the best shape of my life and had the best coaching possible. But the most intriguing part about a marathon is that you never know what will happen race day. Since you are running 26.2 miles, many different variables can come into play.

The race started out great for my running partner and me. In the early miles, we were right on target for a 3:00 finish. I needed a 3:10 to qualify for Boston. At mile sixteen, things changed for the worse. I was feeling a little fatigued. My training partner started to pull away from me, and I had a hard time catching up with him. He had never beaten me in a race so this was not a good sign. This was the turning point of the race. It was a crucial time for positive self talk. All of those negative thoughts started to jump into my mind, such as "I can't do this," and "Why did I do all of this training for the race." I will never forget thinking to myself: "Here I am at mile sixteen, with ten miles to go, and I'm already running on an empty tank."

I immediately cancelled my negative thoughts and went into my positive self-talk mode. Even though I was not physically one hundred percent, it was important to be one hundred percent mentally. I started to think about how much training and time I put into this for the last ten months. I thought about all those mornings I woke up at 5:00 a.m. and did half-mile repeats. The deciding factor that made all the difference was my inner dialog. I started to tell myself: "I can do it." "I feel strong." "I am the best." I gave my brain every positive message imaginable. Sure enough, things started to turn around for me. I continued with this positive self-talk the final ten miles of the race. I finished with a time of 3:07 and qualified for the Boston Marathon! My dream came true! If it weren't for the affirmations before the race, and the positive self talk during the race, I don't think I would have accomplished my goal.

> *"Our subconscious minds have no sense of humor,*
> *play no jokes and cannot tell the difference*
> *between reality and an imagined thought or image.*
> *What we continually think about eventually*
> *will manifest in our lives."*
>
> — SIDNEY MADWED

Visualization and affirmations have been used for years by many many people and are very powerful tools. Start today to put these into action, and you will not be disappointed with the results. Dreams you thought were impossible now can become a reality!

"Persist and persevere, and you will find most things that are attainable, possible."

– LORD CHESTERFIELD

CHAPTER FIVE

Persistence

"Lots of people limit their possibilities by giving up easily. Never tell yourself this is too much for me. It's no use. I can't go on. If you do you're licked, and by your own thinking too. Keep believing and keep on keeping on."

— NORMAN VINCENT PEALE

One of the most valuable traits I have developed over the years is persistence. Persistence was one of the biggest reasons I was able to accomplish my dream of getting to Boston and running the marathon. There were many times when I wanted to give up, but I never took my focus off of my dream. It took twelve long years to accomplish my goal of running in Boston, but I never gave up!

One of my favorite and most inspirational stories relating to persistence is about Colonel Sanders, the founder of Kentucky

Fried Chicken. At the age of 62, after a long and varied career, he had lost his entire net worth and was reduced to living only on Social Security benefits. Confident of the quality of his fried chicken, the Colonel devoted himself to the chicken franchising business, traveling across the country by car from restaurant to restaurant, cooking batches of chicken for restaurant owners and their employees. He was rejected over one thousand times! It was on his one thousand and ninth try when finally someone said "yes" to his dream and the rest is history. The majority of people would have given up after one or two rejections. Colonel Sanders believed in himself and his recipe and would not get discouraged.

Persistence can be applied to all areas of your life. I have been in sales for over twenty years. Persistence is the word that best describes why I have been successful. Think about these statistics:

* **48%** of sales people quit after the first call.

* **24%** quit after the second call.

* **12%** quit after the third call.

* **6%** quit after the fourth call.

* **10%** quit after the fifth call.

Eighty-one percent of sales are made after the fourth call when 90% of sales people have quit calling. The most successful sales people are those who keep persisting and will not take no for an answer. Most of my best customers over the years have thanked me for my persistence! Believe it or not, many people really do appreciate a persistent person. If you truly believe in yourself and your product or service, it will be very hard for clients to say no.

> *"If I had to select the most valuable quality, the most vital personal characteristic that I regard as being most highly correlated with success, whatever the field, I would pick the traits of persistence, coupled with determination. The will to endure to the end, to get knocked down seventy times and get up off the floor saying, 'Here comes number seventy-one.'"*

> – RICHARD M. DEVOS

Why do most sales people quit? The fear factors come into play again: the fear of rejection, fear of being too pushy, fear of loss, etc. But the main reason why sales people quit working on a sales opportunity is they lack discipline and persistence. Do you think Colonel Harland Sanders would have made a good sales person? Most people are born with the ability to be persistent. When we are young children, we are not afraid to ask for what we want. If you understand young children, they are uninhibited about what they want. They see another child who is doing something they want to do, and they simply ask: "Can I play that too?" They have not suffered rejection and trained their neural pathways to expect rejection. This allows them to pursue their wants and needs without fear. Unfortunately over the years, because of fear and other factors, we lose our persistence.

One story I like about persistence is about the first man to reach the top of Mt. Everest. In 1952, Edmund Hillary attempted to climb Mt. Everest, the highest mountain on earth — 29,000 feet straight up. A few weeks after his failed attempt, he was asked to address a group in England. Hillary walked to the edge of the stage, made a fist and pointed at a picture of the mountain. He said in a loud voice, "Mount Everest, you beat me the first time, but I'll beat you the next time because you've grown all you are going to grow....but I'm still growing!" On May 29, only one year later, Edmund Hillary succeeded in becoming the first man to climb Mt. Everest.

If you study successful people, you will find they have had many more failures than successes. Another old saying says that whenever you fail you are that much closer to success. For example, Walt Disney was turned down 302 times before he got the financing for his dream of creating the happiest place on earth. Millions of people have enjoyed Disneyland and Disney World because he never gave up on his dream and persisted until the very end. Thomas Edison said many of life's failures occur because people didn't realize how close they were to success when they gave up. Success is right on the other side of failure.

A great short story that illustrates this is by Napoleon Hill, author of the book <u>Think and Grow Rich</u>. There he tells of a man named Mr. Darby who stopped drilling for gold when he could not pick up the gold vein anymore. He sold the machinery to a junk man and went home. The junk man continued drilling and found the vein just three feet short from where Mr. Darby had stopped drilling. A man is not finished when he is defeated. He is finished when he quits. The most successful people "keep on keeping on" in tough times and never give up!

Changing your mindset is extremely important when it comes to persistence. You need to silence that little doubting man on your shoulder that says you can't do it and you have had enough. Condition your mind so you will never give up. Get rid of any thoughts that don't support you. My sister-in-law had attempted and was forced to give up her first marathon attempt at mile sixteen. A seasoned runner, she decided afterwards that a distance that long was not within her capabilities. Thirteen years later she decided to stop making excuses and give the marathon another try. She developed a plan and stuck with it. During the most difficult of her long runs, the 18 miler, she faced her mental and physical fears of running longer than she had ever run. Around seventeen miles she wanted to quit. Negative thoughts swirled through her head. She said the thing that got her through that run was a line she heard in a documentary about the 1980 US Olympic Hockey Team. Coach Herb Brooks said to his team before the last big game that the players would "take it to their grave…" if they didn't get out there and fight for what they deserved. She did not want to fail. She worked her plan, persisted, and she not only completed her 18 miler, she comfortably finished her first marathon in a little over four hours.

It is important to read stories about individuals who have succeeded by persevering no matter what it took. Talk to as many people as possible who you consider successes with their chosen aspirations. The more reference points you have on persistence, the more you will be able to persevere when the going gets tough and you encounter road blocks. I read a passage on the Mongol Emperor, Tamerlane, and was inspired by an example of persistence which he observed in nature. At one point, his army was routed and Tamerlane lay hidden in a deserted manger. He lay there, desperate and dejected. He observed an ant trying to carry a grain of corn over a perpendicular wall. The kernel was larger than the ant itself. Sixty-nine times the ant tried to carry it up the wall. Sixty-nine times it fell back. On the seventieth try, it pushed the kernel over the top. Tamerlane was very inspired by this ant's persistence. He reorganized his army and put his enemies to flight.

"Persist and persevere, and you will find most things that are attainable, possible."

— LORD CHESTERFIELD

Ray Kroc, the founder of McDonald's, is a classic testimonial to how one great idea along with hard work and perseverance pay off. Kroc was always looking for that "right idea." He had many different careers: paper cup salesman, real estate broker, piano player, and milk shake mixer salesman, but he believed in the saying that "one good idea can make you a fortune." When he was fifty-two years old, he came up with the idea of McDonald's. He had to mortgage his home and borrow quite a bit of money. He opened his first McDonald's in 1955, and it is still an extremely profitable business today. The key to his success was that he never lost faith in himself and kept on persevering. He also had many health problems but that did not stop him. His one great idea and perseverance were the important ingredients to his success.

Ray Kroc had a simple formula for success:

1. Never give up.

2. Always persevere.

3. Don't forget #1.

The more you can consistently develop the habit of persistence the more success you will have in your life.

58 || BOSTON MARATHON OR BUST

Napoleon Hill has put together four simple steps to strengthen your persistence. He recommends developing the following:

1. A definite purpose backed by burning desire for its fulfillment.

2. A definite plan, expressed in continuous action.

3. A mind closed tightly against all negative and discouraging influences, including negative suggestions of relatives, friends and acquaintances.

4. A friendly alliance with one or more persons who will encourage you to follow through with both plan and purpose.

When things go wrong, as they sometimes will
When the road you're trudging seems all up hill

When funds are low and the debts are high
And you want to smile, but you have to sigh

When care is pressing you down a bit
Rest, if you must, but don't you quit

Life is queer with its twists and turns
As every one of us sometimes learns

And many a failure turns about
When he might have won had he stuck it out

Don't give up though the pace seems slow –
You may succeed with another blow

Success is failure turned inside out –
The silver tint of the clouds of doubt

And you never can tell how close you are
It may be near when it seems so far

So stick to the fight when you're hardest hit –
It's when things seem worst that you must not quit

– AUTHOR UNKNOWN

"Why should I clutter my mind with general information when I have men around me who can supply any knowledge I need?"

— HENRY FORD

CHAPTER SIX

Find a Mentor or Coach

Finding a mentor or coach was one of the best decisions I made in my attempt to accomplish my dream of qualifying for and then running in Boston. In my early attempts, I tried to plan and train on my own. Year after year, I was just a couple of minutes short of the qualifying time. Finally, my inspiration presented itself. As I mentioned earlier, April, 1996, was to be the 100th running of the Boston Marathon. For marathoners this was a once-in-a-life-time event that you did not want to miss! I really wanted to run this special Boston Marathon. I wanted it so badly that I hired a coach.

I live in Boulder, Colorado alongside many world class athletes. I was lucky enough to hire a former Olympian who, at one time, was one of the best marathoners in the world. He had run Boston before, so he knew what I was up against. I told him about my dream and what I wanted to accomplish. So we worked out a game plan and then put that plan into action.

Experience

When you are looking for a coach or mentor, seek out someone who has already accomplished what you are trying to achieve. A coach who is experienced in what you wish to achieve will be able to share with you insights and strategies you can use to get results. They can give you decades of wisdom in each coaching session.

The coach I found was someone who already had run Boston with an outstanding finishing time. Learning from someone else's experience can save you years of hard and sometimes futile work and keep you focused. My coach's past experiences became invaluable to me. He gave me many insights, both physical and mental, that helped me achieve my dream. Keep in mind that a good coach usually has been coached themselves. They will bring not only their personal experience to the table, but they will also incorporate all that they learned from other people's experiences.

Learn from their insight

Immediately, this coach was able to share his insight and correct a flaw in a core element of what I had thought was a sound training plan. Here was my mistake. Over the years I had chosen marathons that are scenic but hilly, such as the Big Sur International and the Catalina Island Marathons. Big Sur is considered one of the most beautiful marathon courses in the world. If you were to do just one marathon in your lifetime, this is the one. But for a potential Boston qualifier, this was not a good choice. Big Sur is a hilly course and you can count on adding about 15 minutes to your normal marathon finishing time. The first thing we did together was choose a marathon which had a fast, flat course.

The example above is simplistic, but it shows how, even if you have life experiences, hiring an experienced and knowledgeable coach can bring immediate as well as long-term benefits. When I look back, I should have hired a coach for my first marathon. But as we all know, "hind-sight is 20/20." You can hire a coach for many different areas in your life. For example you can hire a career, business or financial coach to help take you to the "next level." Some of the wealthiest people in the world have had a coach or mentor. This is one of the best-kept secrets of the rich.

> *"I have about concluded that wealth is a state of mind, and that anyone can acquire a wealthy state of mind by thinking rich thoughts."*
>
> – ANDREW YOUNG

GET THAT MIND SET

The mental aspect of coaching is a key element to helping people achieve their goals. When selecting a coach, that person must be someone who will help you break through your limiting fears and beliefs. As I mentioned, I had a deep belief that I could run the qualifying time, but I kept hitting a wall at mile 20. With the expert coaching I received, I was able to knock down that wall that kept showing up at all the previous marathons.

"We have nothing to fear but fear itself."

— Franklin D. Roosevelt

Accountability

There are many people who have great ideas and dreams but never get to live them because of their lack of action and follow-through. In one of Wayne Dyer's books, there is a chapter called "Don't Die with the Music Still Inside of You." Dr. Dyer says that you should listen to your music and do what you know you have to do to feel whole, to feel complete, and to feel as if you are fulfilling your destiny. An enormous benefit of hiring a coach is that person helps you to find your music and make it real by holding you accountable on a daily basis for the results of your plan.

This was of great benefit to me. I have always been disciplined, but meeting with my coach on a weekly basis helped me get focused and clear about my goals and workouts. I remember getting up at 5:00 in the morning and going to the track to do half-mile repeats. This is not easy, but when you have a coach reviewing, critiquing, and encouraging you, it holds you accountable and brings out new motivation. This helps you break out of your comfort zone.

"With every disciplined effort there is
a multiple reward."

– JIM ROHN

COMFORT ZONES

Settling into a comfort zone is a trap that many people fall into. For many years, I was very comfortable with my own training program and was in my comfort zone. When I hired my coach, I broke through this comfort zone in a very short time. The result was achieving my goal very quickly. You need to ask yourself: are you in your comfort zone? Is it time to push yourself a little? A great quote I came across said "Get comfortable with being uncomfortable." When we are in our comfort zone, we are confident, happy and feel relaxed without anxiety and stress. A coach will help you challenge yourself and accept the discomfort in order to grow.

DEVELOP A PLAN

A good coach will help you to create a clear and focused plan. With his or her help, you can set very detailed and clear goals to help you achieve just about any dream you might have. My marathon coach broke down the 26.2 mile course into individual miles. We then decided upon the times needed for each mile. I not only wrote all of them down, but I visualized each mile time as well. In addition he had me visualize the all-important finishing clock with the time I need to qualify. Remember, clarity is power.

I read a great story about clarity a couple of years ago. It was about a man named Bunker Hunt. He rose from being a bankrupt cotton farmer in the 1930s to a multi-billionaire when he died in the 1970s. Mr. Hunt was once asked during a TV interview what advice he could give to others who wanted to be financially successful. He responded by saying that it's not terribly difficult to be successful; only two things are required. First, you must decide exactly what it is you want to accomplish. Most people never do that in their entire lives. And second, you must determine what price you'll have to pay to get it, and then resolve to pay that price. This story illustrates how important it is to have clear goals, to know exactly what it is you want, and to know how to get there.

CAN'T I JUST GET A GOOD BOOK?

You may ask: "What about all the resources you can get at your local bookstore or library? Can I substitute those for a coach?"

You can listen to all tapes, read books, and go to seminars, but remember, that material is geared toward the general population or a large group of similar like-minded people. It is designed to reach the maximum number of people at one time or in one printing. There are times in your life when you will have a need greater than can be met by those resources. That is the time when an expert can help you individually shift your belief system and help you sort out your fears and doubts. That is the time to hire a coach.

It should be your goal not to go to the grave with the music still in you. Open that business you always wanted to start. Move to that farm you always dreamed about. The key is take action. Remember —every great undertaking, accomplishment, and breakthrough all begins with that all-important dream. Then, you need to take action. The bottom line is that by hiring a coach, I was able to achieve my dream that had escaped me for over twelve years.

BUT I LOSE MOTIVATION....

When you are trying to accomplish a goal on your own, it can be difficult sometimes to keep yourself motivated. Through periodic accountability, an experienced coach will see when you are losing your "fire" and will utilize techniques to keep you on track toward accomplishing your goals. Running a marathon takes three to four months of continuous training. There were many times I was lacking in focus and motivation, but my coach worked with me and turned that around very quickly.

> *"Why should I clutter my mind with general information when I have men around me who can supply any knowledge I need?"*

> – Henry Ford

How can I spot a good coach?

Here are some helpful tips when you are looking to find a coach. Dr. Matt Starcevich, Ph.D., has come up with ten great questions to see if your coach passes the test! Answer yes or no to the following questions.

1. The coach sees you as trustworthy, sincere and willing to learn.

2. The coach has a unique perspective or insight to offer.

3. The coach is willing to give of himself or herself and help others.

4. The coach is easy to talk to and be trusted. You don't feel vulnerable.

5. The coach wants to see you succeed.

6. The coach is a teacher, willing to help others grow and develop.

7. The coach expects to learn something during your time together.

8. The coach believes that you should grow out of the need for his/her help. He/she never uses phrases like "You need me" or "I can help you get ahead."

9. The coach believes that you need to struggle and find your own way and never would say, "I know best."

10. You have a good feeling about working with this coach

If you can answer "yes" to these ten questions, then you have found the perfect coach.

In summary, hiring a coach will be one of the best decisions you can make in your life. It will help you reach your dreams and help you live an extraordinary life. I sincerely believe whatever you spend on coaching will come back to you tenfold. In the last three months, I have hired three different coaches and have benefited greatly. I hired a Ph.D. in nutrition as my nutritional/ health coach. She is an expert in her field and I have learned so many great things. Health is wealth. I have also hired two business coaches that have been terrific. I have accomplished more in the last three months with these coaches than I have in the last year trying to do things alone.

"The potential of the average person is like a huge ocean unsailed, a new continent unexplored, a world of possibilities waiting to be released and channeled toward some great good."

– BRIAN TRACY

"There is doing and not doing.

There is no such thing as trying."

— **Scott Armstrong**

Conclusion

ell, the easy part is over. You've read the book. Now what?

The stages of the success plan are not magical. Simply by reading them, they will not happen. This is a self-help book, not a magic wand. You must now DO SOMETHING with what you have learned.

THE 24 HOUR CHALLENGE

If you are truly serious about reaching your dream take the advice of Paul Jackson, who gave us the formula for wisdom. His simple action plan can get you moving in the right direction.

Here it is. Use this statement to motivate you and to give you an action plan that can be repeated every day of your life.

"Within the next 24 hours,
I will _____ which will
move me one step closer to my goal."

The blank is filled in with something that you actually DO. It is an action step. It is measurable. It is one step closer to your dream. It is something you can share with someone who will make you accountable. It is a progress report of your journey to your goal. It is one step toward a target that must be reached in order to fulfill your dream. It is motivation.

This simple 24-hour declarative statement repeated 365 days a year will have you moving, accomplishing, and celebrating in no time at all.

Are you up to the challenge? Complete this Sentence.

"Within the next 24 hours
I will _____."

The basic steps in the success plan are proven to be effective. Individuals will find some of the steps easy to do and some will be more difficult. Some of the steps you already do, others are new to you. In combination, they are a proven success plan.

❋ ***Understand*** the Power of Beliefs

❋ ***Set*** Your Goals

❋ *Practice* Visualization

❋ *Repeat* Your Affirmations

❋ *Practice* Persistence

❋ *Find* a Mentor or Coach

Take some time right now to do some reflection on the contents of the book and the steps of the plan in particular.

Consider the following reflective exercises. Write your answers on a sheet of paper. This helps you focus and will get you actually doing something rather than just thinking about it.

1. If I rank-ordered these steps of the plan in the order of how I see them as important, from most important to least important, my list would be…

2. The step(s) on the list I am already most comfortable with are…

3. The step(s) on the list I will likely find most difficult to achieve would be…

4. In giving some thought to possible mentors/coaches, I believe my list could include…

5. Of all the resources available to me to expand on these steps and help me reach my dream, I would start with…

6. I need to find out more about…

7. My dream is… My goals along the way to accomplishing my dream will include…

8. If I am truly serious about achieving my dream I will begin the process today by…

Putting your thoughts on paper makes the dream more of a reality. Sharing your dream with others gives you the impetus to get started.

Accomplishing small goals toward your big dream will keep you moving.

Visualizing yourself in a "dream come true" situation will carry you through the tough times.

> *"There is doing and not doing.*
> *There is no such thing as trying."*

You cannot "try" to make your dream come true. It is time to act!

Scott Armstrong
http://www.BoulderCoachingAcademy.com
Scott@BoulderCoachingAcademy.com

ABOUT THE AUTHOR

SCOTT SHARP ARMSTRONG IS CONSIDERED ONE OF THE top success coaches in the United States. Through his company, Boulder Coaching Academy, he helps people transform their lives.

Scott says his mission is to embody and promote all aspects of a healthy lifestyle while coaching people to discover how to achieve their own goals and dreams. He has coached clients worldwide — from the United States, Canada, England, Ireland, Australia and New Zealand, to Switzerland, Sweden, South Africa, Denmark, Iceland, Czechoslovakia, Trinidad, and Curacao.

Scott's clients are not only geographically diverse, they also come from a broad experiential and occupational spectrum, encompassing retirees looking for a new direction in life, as well as all types of top-level executives, salespeople, teachers, doctors, lawyers, engineers – even other coaches.

All look to the Boulder Coaching Academy curricula to help them:

- *Break* through self-limiting boundaries

- *Set* and achieve personal and professional goals

- *Acquire* self-assurance, enhance self confidence, gain poise in stressful situations

- *Torpedo* procrastination by learning how to take action – consistently

- *Learn* how to "Dream Big"

- *Design* a life of purpose

- *Recognize* opportunities and seize life's possibilities

He himself has been mentored by some of the world's best personal development teachers, such as Anthony Robbins and Zig Ziglar,

He feels his most influential and life changing event was a four day seminar with Anthony Robbins, which culminated with the fire-walk experience. Completing the Robbins program helped him raise his "mental game" to an entirely new level.

He values qualifying for and running in the Boston Marathon as one of his greatest personal success stories, which led him to incorporate the story into his book, *Boston Marathon or Bust*.

Scott lives with his beautiful wife, Sarah, by a lake in the foothills of Boulder, Colorado, where he also bases Boulder Coaching Academy.

BONUS!!

VISIT SCOTT'S WEBSITE, BOSTONMARATHONORBUST.COM, and download your free *Boston Marathon or Bust* workbook!

This workbook was created for you, to help accelerate your success plan even faster!

It gives you space to work through all the parts of the plan outlined in this book. You will be taken through a goal setting workshop where you will learn how to write your goals and sub goals clearly and concisely. You will write down your daily affirmations, learn to establish an "attitude of gratitude," and ***much*** more.

Get the results you desire! Visit Scott on the web today!

Printed in the USA
CPSIA information can be obtained
at www.ICGtesting.com
JSHW082221140824
68134JS00015B/673

9 781600 372452